Juvenile and Pedantic

By K. W. Kibbe

Author's Note

It may seem ostensibly in this book that I generalize certain types of people by race or country of origin. I admit that I do generalize people on certain issues like hate but that is because it is acceptable because most people that hold certain aspects like race or gender in common usually have the same opinions, but as always, there are exceptions to this stereotyping.

Also, I do not care for your stories on why you do certain actions; I do not care if there was something that had happened to you that supposedly makes your opinion more qualified, verified, and just than mine because your opinion shouldn't be more valid than mine on political opinions because we both are people and we both can have opinion; what makes the difference is the fact of how well I can defend my claim compared to how well you can defend your claim. I do not argue by having degrees or plaques on my walls, rather by using pragmatism and ideology.

As an example: if a doctor would tell me to take medicine for a headache, I probably would, not because of his doctor's degree in medical science, but because there's no reason not to when I've observed the effects of medicine on others. Having a degree stating your specialty only narrows your sight in an event to your specific field and how it will affect that field specifically instead of looking at the grand picture.

This is my first book, showing my political opinions on controversial issues like the L.G.B.T. Community, Abortion, Prayer in School, feminism, etc. I know, pretty lamb for a kid to write about these topics, but this would be a start for a newbie to get into politics with a relatively cheap book to just challenge what they think they know, test the foundation of their beliefs before going somewhere radical like the Communist Manifesto.

On Culture

There are many diverse types of cultures, mainly in three quasi-independent parts: religious culture, racial culture, and geographical culture. Often, they are all misunderstood and confused with each other. An example of this is the confusion in World War II that the Jews are a race of people instead of followers of religion; this effect and confusion has still leaked into today's culture with increasing spikes of anti-semitism recently, along with Islamophobia being considered racist.

It is a theory that multiculturalism forces a form of Nazism, which can happen in some scenarios. However, in the majority of these scenarios, this will not happen. As stated before, there are three types of culture. Religious culture is based on stereotypes of its members. Usually, in history, people base stereotypes on the actions of a few of its followers and the common face-value of the religion itself, along with the other two types of culture.

The common anti-Semitic belief of what Jews look like are men or women with curly, dark hair, long noses, and seem to be more greedy than the average person.

The Islamophobic stereotype is a man with a turban that beats his wives, kills people because of his religion, and are complete terrorists. The Muslim extremist groups like the Taliban, Isis, Al-Qaeda, the Muslim Brotherhood, etc. all invoke a doctrine called the Jihad, which is their struggle for being a Muslim and trying to spread their religion. These cowardly terrorist groups use the Jihad to explain their attacks; they hide behind their religion like spineless children. Once again, you can convert to Islam like you can with Christianity; you don't have to be middle-Eastern to be considered a Muslim -- however, according to Khalifas, only Arabs, people born in the Arabian Peninsula, are considered true Muslims.

The Anti-Christian stereotype is the one I am most commonly associated with because I live in an atheist area as a Christian. This stereotype could come from the atheists that I've known (all of whom tend to be condescending more than I and culturally liberal), even though I was one of them for a while until I decided to look at theology from the point-of-view of a convert. Back to the point! The stereotype is someone who only talks about Jesus and doesn't think for themselves. There's actually a life-experience story that goes with this one. I know this girl who wasn't Christian for the majority of her life, and, all of a sudden, she started acting overly pious, making a public statement of it almost. Props to her for wanting to be a Christian, but by being a stereotype is not the best way to start the process of enlightenment.

The Atheist Stereotype is a person who is not religious at all and is usually an intellectual person, always relating life to science. Most scientists are Atheists, believing only what they prove. Supposedly, they are also bummers, people who spoil the fun in actions. What the atheists don't understand about their science is its roots that stem from the Catholic Church for the first 1,000 years of its existence until the Protestant Reformation. Plus, the Big Bang Theory was created by a priest.

I am a firm believer that anyone can change (I mean, just look at me. I used to be a God-hating Communist who turned into a God-loving Conservative. I've changed so much I had to rewrite this book to better fit my stances). As a convert, I know people can change their religion and belief, so I do not scorn others of a different Creed than I, I rather pray for their prosperity, their conversion, and their safety. In the meantime, I also help them however I can, whether it's by theological discussion or manual labor.

Secondly, there is racial culture, which is the culture that one is a part of because of what race they are. Multiculturalism in this sense brings less biodiversity, which can be harmful, but we can overcome that barrier. Your race often affects the other two cultures and what people think about it. An example: if I am Arabic, then people would assume that I am a Muslim and from the Arabian Peninsula. My parents could be native and I could have been born in Northern Europe and raised a Zoroastrian.

Your race affects how some people view you, whether it be as a possible criminal because your race has a higher crime rate, or if they believe you to be smarter because of your eyes. This won't change, and it sucks, but we've already come a long way where the only racists left that are concerning are the Boomers. Even if there were one race, people would naturally segregate themselves on religion, politics, and other differences. It's what the human brain wants to do, look for differences, so when people do that, know they aren't really racist, they're only natural and probably not a hate group.

For instance, my mother, Bohemian by blood (Bohemia was a country in the modern Eastern European Slavic area that is now the Czech Republic and Slovakia), was hated by an older man when she was in her youth, just because she was a

Bohemian, not even a native one. You must look at all cultural ties and issues logically and rationally to be reasonable: can a person choose where they are from? Their race? Their sex? To these three, the answer is "no", but you can choose your religion; however, you shouldn't have to change your religion: it says so in the First Amendment, which almost all or all European and Asian countries have adopted.

The African-Americans often talk about slavery like we, the whites of America, descendants of the British Colonial folk, owe them something. Some of them are rational and see that we do not, but others don't care for rationality. In the West Indies trade between the 13 British Colonies of America (this was pre-1776) and Africa, we would purchase rum from the West Indies, then sell it to the Africans, who would sell us some slaves of their own kind -- I cannot stress that enough -- and money that they had for the rum. We would then sell the slaves to the West Indies for more rum, and that creates a little economic circle. If the African Americans want someone to blame for their ancestors' suffering, then they should blame the native Africans also.

As stated before, my race also affects where people believe that I was born and what religion I practice. If I were Japanese-American, people would think that I was born in Japan and a part of either Buddhism or Shinto, which, again, could be wrong. Finally, there is the regional culture, which affects the other two cultures and is affected by the other two cultures. There are regions like the Arabian Peninsula, West Africa, Ghetto America, South Pacific, etc. If you are born in the Arabian Peninsula, you are Arabic by race, but your religion doesn't have to Islam or Judaism; it could be Hindu. There is a direct effect on race from the region; using an example based on the one from before, I can be born in the Arabian Peninsula and be considered an Arab, but my native race could be Polish. Then I'd be a Polish Arab.

The area of India is hugely multicultural: they have Pakistani, Indian, Tibetan, Nepali, etc. all in that area. In the 1950s and 1960s, India was being carved up by Britain to create a new Islamic state of Pakistan where over 600,000 people died after Pakistan was created. There are also more than 1 billion people in India, which also helps with the racial ties. India was ruled by Britain until the time of Mahatma Gandhi. There was also a tremendously thick trade between the Europeans and the Indians, by sea and by land (Silk Trade).

There are also regions in China that are so diverse, fresh with the scars of the Spheres of Influence and the memory of the Opium Trade Wars and Hong Kong in their minds. There is also a diverse West-Coast U.S.A. with a huge Chinese influence in California, the German influence in the Midwest Great Plains, the Mexican influence in Southeastern U.S.A., etc.

People are often criticized for being uncultured. Everyone should know something about their country, like how almost all U.S. citizens know about the American Revolution, or France knowing about Napoleon Bonaparte, etc., but it's not their responsibility to know about other cultures and submit to cultural appropriation.

The nation's culture helps to improve morale and thought about the nation and its citizens, along with their -- the citizens -- ideal of nationalism. When in a state of war, a country will almost always try to increase nationalism in its citizens: if you lose your people in a state of war, then you lost the war completely. Who pays taxes for the war effort? Who goes and fights sometimes an ocean away? The people. They are the key to success.

It is seen by many people that society pressures people to change the way that they look. For an example, the characteristics that men should have are strong, tall, fast, and muscular; the characteristics that women should have -- by how people believe society forces them to be -- are skinny and Coca-Cola Bottle-shaped. Often, what people do to combat these pressures is to say that those people do not exist, which is idiotic; just because you don't respond well to pressure does not make it right to say that an entire group of people does not exist. Are there women and men that are affected by society's standards? Yes. Should we change ourselves? In most cases, no (and I say "most cases" because if you are obese or you are something else negative to your body and it is in your power to change, you really should. Be the Ubermensch!).

The most common combat among the women against the supposed "society image pressure" is the statement "Those aren't real women. Real women have curves," which, again, denounce an entire group of people. I know a person named Autumn Dulong, and she has a lot of stress from school and society, and on this issue of pressure for women to fit a certain standard, she says that "women are more pressured in society because of all the advertisement promoting sex." Some people may ask "why is she qualified to make this statement? Why should we listen?" She does not have a degree in psychology, sociology, or a degree in any professional field at all. She was a classmate of mine last year. She is qualified to make this statement because she can have an opinion on this situation and she understands the pressure.

Generally, men do not complain about the "society image pressure", nor do they really care. They just accept it and continue on with life. As a male, I can tell you that I don't really care for the bodies of other people, nor do I feel stressed over my body. It may be something biological for men to not worry about their body or it may be something that society actually has created, but to me, it seems biological.

Many people, usually leaning to the left, claim that the United States is still a racist society and a racist country because it was found by racist, slave-owning men. To this absurd claim, I glance over to the Civil Rights Act of 1964. This Act was passed in President Lyndon B. Johnson's term in office from 1964 to 1968 because of President J.F.K.'s assassination in 1963. What the Civil Rights Act of 1964 had done was end segregation in public areas like metros and schools, and banned employment discrimination on the terms of an individual's sex, race, color, or nationality. There is literally no law saying that only white people can do this action, nor any law specializing women, or minorities.

There is no such existence as "Rape Culture" here in the United States. There may be in Third world countries like Ethiopia and Saudi Arabia, but that horrid, evil culture is nonexistent because we know that rape is a terrible, gruesome, unnatural act and those rapists are, in turn, punished by Capital punishment or by life-long sentences in jail, or even a shorter jail time in turn for voluntary castration.

What exactly is the definition of "rape culture"? According to Marshall University,

> "Rape Culture is an environment in which rape is prevalent and in which sexual violence against women is normalized and excused in the media and popular culture. Rape culture is perpetuated through the use of misogynistic language, the objectification of women's bodies, and the glamorization of sexual violence, thereby creating a society that disregards women's rights and safety."

When people say that rape culture exists in the United States, they also follow the myth that one-tenth of all rape crimes are reported. If we don't know that they happen, then how do we know that the number that we're missing is nine-tenths? You may argue that the number will be higher than that, but it isn't because people report crimes that are personal to them the most. This also makes it so the

Harvard Campus is more dangerous to women than Detroit.

In what way is the United States normalizing sexual harassment against women? We put rapists in prison for their crime. There aren't any media where people just get raped, the rapists are then persecuted and sent to prison, and in my entire life, I've never heard anyone joke about rape before. Not once. Explain to me how rape is being promoted, or that sexual harassment is being normalized in the United States.

This is not enough to match the extremes of this type of crime! If anyone is to commit rape and it can be proven with evidence, then we should chemically castrate or have an oophorectomy done on the rapist forcefully, then they should continue to receive twenty years in prison.

On Spirituality

According to historians, there are five Major World Religions: Hinduism, -- an especially ethnic religion in the Indian Peninsula -- Judaism, -- a religion with 14 million followers, yet is still facing massive prejudice -- Buddhism, -- an Indi-Asian religion that is retro in the U.S. -- Christianity, -- the most prosperous religion -- and Islam -- the most common religion second to Christianity, mainly located in the Arabic Penninsula and Africa. There are many other religions like Taoism, Sikhism, Confucianism, and Jainism, just to name a few. Many people have their own personal beliefs about spirituality; they may be theists, for an example. Another example is from personal experience; my father was raised as a Free Methodist by his grandmother until he was around the age of eleven years. When he was eleven, he was forced to be one of Jehovah's Witnesses by his parents. Later, when he was away from his parents, he was back to being a Free Methodist, except he was now a theist -- not an atheist. Atheism and Theism are two extremely different faiths -- at this point in his life. What he believes in is that there is a higher being and that there is/was Jesus Christ; that is his personal belief on spirituality.

When stating the five Major World Religions in the last paragraph, I placed them in the order of occurrence, from oldest to newest (Hinduism is the oldest and Islam is the most recent). It's important to categorize these religions by most ancient to most recent, not only because of the history, but also because of how the religion's age effects itself; the most qualified example is the three Abrahamic religions: Judaism, Christianity, and Islam. Christianity is based on Judaism, and Islam on Christianity. There will be a major debate happening over this subject based on heredity, importance, and religious roles, so I'm going to avoid it for now.

Hinduism is the most ancient of the five Major World Religions, being around 4,000 years old. Hinduism is polytheistic -- one of the only lasting polytheistic religions -- with their main Gods Brahma, Vishnu, and Shiva. Those are the supreme Gods of Hinduism; there are more: many, many more; I find it a tedious task to name them all. In Hinduism, they also believe that there are human forms of Gods and Goddesses called Avatars. Hinduism is a popular belief in the areas of Tibet, India, and many more Eastern-Asian countries.

Judaism is the world's oldest official form of Abrahamic religions and monotheism (later comes Zoroastrianism, a minor Middle-Eastern religion around 2,700 years old). Judaism was formed around 3,900 years ago by my calculations (Moses lived in the Thirteenth century B.C.E., and before him, 400 years had passed since Jacob was brought to Egypt). As stated before, Judaism is monotheistic, which has the belief of one God, often named in Hebrew 'Adonai'. The religious book for the Jews is the Torah. People can also read the Tanakh, which is the Hebrew Old Testament -- if you want to compare it to the Christian Bible. Judaism is a popular belief in Israel, a Middle Eastern country, and the United States.

Buddhism is the "path to enlightenment" in Tibetan. "Buddha" is literally "the enlightened one". Buddhism started around 2,600 years ago with Siddhartha Gautama, the first Buddha. Buddhism can be both polytheistic or monotheistic because it never mentions God anywhere in its teachings. There are few sacred texts for Buddhism, mainly some old unnamed scrolls or written phrases; Buddhism is taught through people and mentors, not through books. Buddhism is a popular belief in Tibet and other far-East Asian countries like Korea and Japan. Buddhism also believes that there are both evil and good spirits and that when a spirit reaches a state of enlightenment, or Nirvana, which you have to be human to reach, the spirit's reincarnation process ends, along with that soul's suffering.

Christianity is the second oldest of Abrahamic religions. Christianity has fully formed around 1700 years ago with the official religion of the Byzantine Empire being Christianity because of Constantine. Christianity, in general, focuses on the belief that Jesus Christ is the son of the Jewish God, the Messiah, and the Third and final part of the Trinity; of course, not all branches of Christianity agree on these topics, and some don't agree with the main points that I have just established (the Protestants and Catholics come to mind), but, generally, more Christians believe in those three points. The religious book for Christians is the Christian Bible, more specifically their New Testimate. Christianity is a popular belief in Europe and the entire Western Hemisphere.

Now, of course, there is more than one branch of Christianity. One of the biggest and most important branches of Christianity is the Roman Catholics. Most people isolate Catholicism from Christianity; they are one and the same in the sense of being Christianity, just that people see the differences instead of the similarities. There are two main branches of Christianity: Protestants and the

Catholics in the year 1517 (the first split of the Christian Church was between the Catholics in the west of Europe and the Orthodox in the east in 1054). However, there are two smaller groups of protestants who were created relatively recently: the Mormons and the Jehovah's Witnesses. The Mormons are those who believe in an additional testament named "the Book of Mormon" or "Mormon Beliefs", along with the Prophet Joseph Smith and Bringham Young. They were created in 1830. The Jehovah's Witnesses are fundamentalists who believe in the Hebrew/Aramaic Scripture (Old Testament) and the Greek Scripture (New Testament). They also believe that the biblical end is near, along with how God's name is Jehovah. They're an apocalyptic group strict on being sola scriptura, found in the 1870s by Charles Taze Russell who thought Apocalypse was coming in the 1920s because of World War One.

Islam, is the most recent of the five Major World Religions and Abrahamic religions. Islam was created around 1400 years ago with their Prophet Muhammed. Islam, in essence, is based on the study of the Qur'an, along with the review of Hadiths -- sayings from the Muhammed. There are two branches of Islam because of a split in political beliefs. The Islamic belief consists of Muhammad being the final prophet for Allah -- God -- and Jesus is a prophet of Allah and not its son (I use "its" because, in Abrahamic religions, God is naturally a non-physical being that can manifest). Islam is most popular in the areas of North Africa, East Africa, the Middle East, and West Asia; it still maintains some influence in Southern Europe like Spain from the Moors.

There is also another religious group on the rise: the religious group of Atheism. It may offend some people -- Atheists -- that I say Atheism is a religion when it is. Atheism states that the belief that there is no god and that nothing exists unless it can be proven, e.i. Materialists, scientists, etc. They are a religious group because their belief has to do with religion, and they can deny it all they want, but that won't change my mind, nor should it yours.

A counterpart to Atheism is Theism, the belief that there is a god, but it will not interfere with the mortal realm, nor with daily life. Theism itself is the belief in a superior being, or God(s). There are mainly three types of theists: monotheists, believers of a single god, polytheists, believers in many gods, and a new reactionary form of theism that was already stated. Atheists and Theists tend to lean more towards science and tend to work better than an Atheist and a Muslim for obvious reasons. In summary, plain theism is Gnosticism.

Religion teaches morals. We, as a person, prosperous and righteous, should have those morals. A call back to religion is required. As long as religion doesn't harm yourself or others, it should be accepted with open arms and without weapons of prejudice. People also should not put faith over reason; we've tried that before and it was horrible.

The U.S.S.R. and other communist groups tried to root out God in the people's culture to control them better by replacing God with the State. They would go as far as raiding their houses and burning their statues or anything religious.

The people that I debate religion with, I respect. They, for the most part, have religion themselves. For instance, I ask questions to Rabbi Mark S. Golub in New York. I talk to Rabbi Golub about Judaism and all the questions that I have, like "What's the difference between Hasidic Judaism and Orthodox Judaism", and he gave me a great answer the next day; however, I also debate religion with some non-religious people who have a hard time justifying answers for morals, eventually devolving into circular logic. Circular logic is never justifiable, and circular logic has been removed from most theological Christian debates, thanks to mainly Saint Thomas Aquinas.

There is this great political poster used by the U.S.S.R. that states something around the lines of: "Knowledge breaks the chains of slavery." This is true, especially in propaganda. If you know nothing about a topic, when the government makes propaganda, they decide what your opinion on issues can be. Kind of ironic how the U.S.S.R. made a poster against propaganda, huh?

There is this land in the Middle East and it is called Canaan, Israel, Palestine, all these different names for the same thing. Originally, the Jews had this land, but the Muslims had control over this land with the creation of the Ottoman Empire. The Christians did not like this, somewhere around 1150-1200 A.D.E., and so the Christians started a Crusade, or "Holy War" -- an oxymoron -- to claim the Promised Land for the Christians. This continued until around 1330 A.D.E. when the Ninth and final crusade ended. Sadly, none of the Crusades worked in taking back the Holy Land.

Since the State of Israel was established in 1948, the war had begun, and instead of Christians v. Muslims, it was now Jews v. Muslims. From my knowledge, the Israelites aren't going into Palestine, murdering all Muslims that they see, but that is exactly what some Palestines are doing, along with Hamas, who also launches missiles into Israel. Hamas is still doing this, and no-one is helping in Israel's efforts. The Jews were there first, and the claim from the Palestinians about them being kicked off their land seventy-one years ago is idiotic. Since Rome conquered Israel, the Jews didn't have their land anymore, so it is arguable that the Jews were kicked off their land over a millennia ago.

Cults in the sense you and I know them are bad things, like the People's Temple, or Heaven's Gate, or the Manson Family.

Worshipping someone for their holiness as an intercessor is different from believing that they are God themself. An example is the Catholics and their Saints. They do not worship the saints, they ask them to intercede on their behalf. Like the Franciscans, they usually pray to Saint Francis (meaning "to ask") for God to give them the graces he received in his lifetime.

Another example being King David -- surely the new generation must know of him? He defeated and killed the Philistine Champion the Giant Goliath by using stone and sling to knock-out Goliath and then proceeded to use his own sword -- Goliath's -- to cut off Goliath's head. He was praised by King Saul and married his daughter. David then proceeds to -- after he was named King -- to kill all giants.

I am not saying that you shouldn't worship a god with a physical form -- Christianity comes to mind. As long as they are gods, they are gods, no matter their physical or spiritual form. You have a right to be free religiously, and I am not trying to take that away from you, I am trying to stop the Cults of the World.

You have to be able to separate the person from the worshiper. If you have a problem with Islam, it's with Islam and not the Muslims; with Christianity and not the Christians; with Judaism and not the Jews; etc. If you have a problem with the people and not the religion, it would be with Muslims and not Islam; with Christians and not with Christianity; with Jews and not with Judaism; etc. People can have a problem with both, which is the main thing of what happens in society's prejudice.

There is yet another issue: prayer being allowed or forced in school. Prayer in schools was a controversial issue in the 1950s and '60s until it reached the Supreme Court in *Engel v. Vitale* in 1961 where the Supreme Court ruled that State Officials like teachers cannot impose religious views on the students in 1962. The issue started with the Regents Prayer and the school teachers teaching their students how to pray like a Christian.

Two Jewish parents saw their children praying like this and they were upset.

The state of New York had passed a law in 1951 mandating the Regents Prayer to be said after the Pledge of Allegiance. The parents argued that the legalization of such an act was in violation of the Establishment Clause of the First Amendment in the Constitution of the United States, which is "Congress shall make no law respecting an establishment of religion, or prohibiting the free exercise thereof."

Because of the mandate of the Regents Prayer by the State Government, this should be a State-issue, but it violates a federal right and so it was an evolution into the Supreme Court. In all, there were ten parents acting as plaintiffs who challenged the governmental adoption of the Regents Prayer as a mandate to the New York Supreme Court, which would be appealed to the United States Supreme Court. Steven Engel's name was the first of the Plaintiffs and William J. Vitale Jr. was the President of the school board, hence the name "*Engel v. Vitale*".

To first understand the wall between Church and State, we must delve into the history of Church and State, starting with the three motherlands of North America -- England, France, and Spain --

their history of religion, and their colonies in colonial times.

Spain, before 1492, was ruled by a Muslim King Boabdil and aided the Ottoman Empire until the Moors were dethroned in 1429 and a new Monarchy was established on the religion of Catholics. Since Spain was and still is deeply Catholic since before the Colonial Age, Spain made sure that all of its colonists were also Catholics. There was also a codependence between the Government and the Church; the Church would donate money to the Government, and, in turn, the Government protected the Church.

France, at this time, was Roman-Catholic and did the same with the colonists of New France as Spain did with the colonists of New Spain. New France, however, was growing at a stagnant level compared to the other colonies of North America. They still had the same codependence between Government and Church that Spain had.

Lemon v. Kurtzman stated that the government would not give financial aid to schools who will use that money in non-secular ways. It also established jurisprudence of a test to be set on upcoming court cases that claim to violate the Establishment Clause. The test was triple-pronged; it tested whether the law was going toward a secular purpose (in *Lemon v. Kurtzman*, the legislative law was to educate Rhode Island students), whether the law affects religion or not (private schools are dismayed because they are not public schools and does not promote religion), and whether the law creates excessive entanglement between the Church and the State.

The final issue is about religious cults versus cults of personality. Cults of personality are more dangerous than religious cults for one reason: the probability of homicide. Yes, I know about the Manson Murders, but that isn't as large as the homicides committed because of cults of personality. By "Cult of Personality", I mainly mean the almost deification of a political figure, like Joseph Stalin. I've already written an article to the New York Times (back when I was a Commie) about this issue. Here it is, edited to fit better:

> The latin word *"cultus"* means "care", and there is no objective definition of the word "cult", but everyone has some sort of idea of cult, yet no definition tells us where a fanatic or a passion becomes an obsession or cultish, until it reaches the point of killing or being killed, seen in Waco Texas, Heaven's Gate, and all the cults previously named.

In the past, those cults have usually committed suicide (with the exception of the Manson Family), harming only themselves. Heaven's Gate committed suicide in March of 1997, killing 39 people. The Peoples Temple killed themselves in South America, ending the lives of 918 people. When compared to the lives lost from cults of personality, these are relatively few.

Most politics later than the First World War involve politicians who cannot do any wrong - who have a cult of personality. We can see this in Benito Mussolini, Adolf Hitler, Joseph Stalin, Franklin D. Roosevelt, etc. This is a side effect of God and religion being removed from culture. These cults of personality are dangerous, preferring homicide to deal with their issues. Mussolini killed around 800 thousand people; Hitler caused the death of around 12 million people; Stalin killed around 10 million people. These are the dangerous political ones in dictatorships.

FDR had killed no one. He was ascending to dictatorship in his attempts to pack the Supreme Court with Justices who agreed with his political philosophy. This is against the Constitution, and there was already a court case similar to it (*Marbury v. Madison*). FDR himself thought that he was great with his New Deal acts. He tried to establish what is a democratic version of a Single-Party State. If this were to happen, he may have gone mad at anyone who disagreed with him, possibly federally executing them on charges of "High Treason".

Seeing as how many deaths were caused by Cults of Personality under a Dictatorship when compared to the amount of deaths caused by religious cults, we can see that Cults of Personality are more dangerous for the general populous. This stems from homicide compared to suicide: when murdering someone, you have the potential to take more than just one life. Beware the cults of personality in modern politics; instill God and religion back into culture!

Pretty easy to understand when it's put like that, huh? I'm sorry if it's not. It took me a while to come to that conclusion myself.

On Abortion

Abortion has been a controversial issue recently, with the possible reversal on the ruling precedent of *Roe v. Wade* and the Annual March for Life on January 18th in Washington D.C. -- which had an estimated half-million attendees with speakers like Ben Shapiro and Vice President Mike Pence. Abortion was a humongous issue from before the 1940s, arguably a grand issue from revolutionary times, but became more apparent with the Movement of Feminism.

I am Pro-Life, so, obviously, I had listened to as much of it as I could. Taking this issue up with friends, family, and peers, most of them are Pro-Choice and this caused many discussions over months.

First, I talked to my sister, 17-years-old, who believes that it is a woman's right to kill the baby. I've had more arguments with her about this, but she doesn't see the correlation between the argument for slavery compared to the argument for abortion. There is a massive correlation, so do some research. Secondly, I've talked to a peer in 9th Grade (who I'll be addressing as "Ms. D") who also is Pro-Choice -- her best friend, however, is Pro-Life. Ms. D listens to what I have to say, not interrupting, and I do the same; she doesn't want to argue, however. Thirdly, I've talked to several of my friends, all a year junior, senior, or the same age, and they have exceptions with abortion, all being summed up in three main points:

1. In the case of Rape, abortion should be allowed.
2. If the family is financially unstable, having the child be born in poverty is cruel.
3. The Court Case of *Roe v. Wade*.

The first point happens less than 1% of the annual abortion amount in the United States of America; the issue that you've been raped and the fact that you're pregnant are two separate issues. Rape is evil. Convict the supposed raper successfully (DNA tests with the child is the best way to prove the rape) and either castrate or kill the raper lawfully. It is still wrong to kill a baby. This is the exact same stance as Ben Shapiro's opinion on abortion. Another action that could be used to combat this issue, since most of the rapists are male, is to allow women to use whatever handgun they want (within reason) and train them with these weapons so that if she is being raped she can shoot the rapist.

Rape is a capital crime and it deserves to be. Abortion should be considered a capital punishment for manslaughter. Also, a life created from rape is equal to a life created consensually. We all, for the most part, are born without physical or mental disabilities: it's the choices that we make in our life that determines how good or bad we are in people. Doubtless, killing a living being is an act for vile people.

For the second point, financially unstable, almost no-one is wealthy enough to have children and still be above the poverty rate; it's only the people like President Trump, Bill Gates, etc. who could afford to have children. It's people's right to have children. This point is an idiotic, debris defense to my argument. Overpopulation can cause higher poverty rates, but not in the correct system. Pregnancy happens to more than just the lower class, it happens to all people no matter what wage you get paid. Rockefeller had children just as the poor peasant in a farm area.

Finally, there is the Case of Roe v. Wade. In the Case of Roe v. Wade, the Supreme Court of the United States of America stated that abortion is legal to an extent (variable in different States). They argue: "It's legal in Roe v. Wade". My response to that: just because it is legal doesn't mean that it is right; slavery was legal; sterilization of the mentally ill was legal until it was reversed with *Skinner v. Oklahoma.*

Women also somehow accidentally get pregnant. I do not understand how this happens. We are creatures that reproduce sexually, which means that you must have a partner of the opposite sex. I do not understand, nor does anyone, how women can accidentally get pregnant. You have to deal with the consequences of your actions. This is the real world. Everyone else has to as well.

Leading up to Roe v. Wade, there was this massive call for the reform of laws on the grounds of abortion, mainly in the New England and the Southern States like Connecticut, New York, Texas, Louisiana, Arizona, etc. Due to these massive reform calls and the new Feminist Movement (see later in "On Gender"), the women -- specifically two Feminist women named Linda Coffee and Sarah Weddington, not originally from the South -- and started to get court trials in the Southern states like Texas -- which is the home for Roe v. Wade -- and Arizona even though their court law said that the prosecutors must have some sort of stake in what they propose (in this case, the women must be pregnant). Neither Coffee nor Weddington was pregnant, and Texas didn't accept abortion at the time, even in the case of rape. Coffee and Weddington relied heavily on the privacy laws of Griswold and reference to the Ninth and Fourteenth Amendments. By the end of the 1970s, almost all states of importance were passing reform laws on abortion; all states but two: Texas and Georgia. There would be a major controversy.

In the court case of Roe v. Wade, Roe, the prosecutor against the State of Texas, said that abortion should be legal because of the First Amendment, the Fourth Amendment, the Ninth Amendment, and the Fourteenth Amendment. It's not a religious action to not have an abortion, it's just the morally right thing to do as a human; you can feel safe with a baby; it was already a State issue and the law was against abortion except in the case of rape; you are denying life when you get an abortion. Regardless of if it needs due process, murder is a Federal Crime; it just so happens that abortion is the legalized killing and not unlawful, so it's not considered murder.

The result of Roe v. Wade was the doctrine that abortion laws are to be set by the individual states in their constitution. Most states allow for First Trimester Abortions without question, and then set certain restrictions on Second Trimester

Abortions and no state allows for Third Trimester Abortion unless the health of the mother or the life of the mother is at risk with the pregnancy. This is called the "Blackmun's Trimester Framework" because Justice Blackmun wrote the Supreme Court's opinion for the majority suggesting the framework on abortion restrictions from what trimester of the pregnancy the woman is at.

The case of Roe v. Wade promoted abortion because, in the following decades, we see that the abortion rate had sharply increased from 615,831 in 1973 to 1,429,247 in 1990; that is more than a one-hundred percent increase! After 1990, however, the abortion rate has been steadily back down to around half a million (638,169 in 2015) but then have been rising to around 1,000,000 again.

Legalizing abortion has had an effect on all of us, demoralizing the country. Now, we think whatever to a life dying by human choice. In the 1920s, there were an estimated 200,000 to 1,000,000 abortions yearly. When abortion became legalized in England, the average family size was from around eight children to less than four. That's a humongous change in the size of the Family. Another piece of evidence that the legalization of abortion contributed to a drop in morals is that about half of the pregnancies in the U.S. are unintentional.

If abortion were to be made illegal, morals would increase sharply before the 1920s, and so would family size. It would also eliminate the amount of Prostitution in the United States because the prostitutes wouldn't be able to get the abortion legally, so they would use other methods like various birth control methods like protection and douching, but also illegal abortions that will probably result in their death or immediate decline of health. This will be a risk that they'll be taking; either danger your health severely or don't be a prostitute.

Additionally, there's the argument that the unborn child is not a living thing. To this issue, we turn to Biology, the study of the living world. In Biology, there is a system of 8 characteristics that all living things hold common.

1. Made of cells
2. Reproduce
3. Based on a Universal Genetic Code
4. Grow and develop
5. Obtain and use materials and energy
6. Respond to their environment
7. Maintain homeostasis
8. As a group, they change over time (evolve)

If you compare baby development inside the womb, they follow all of these characteristics. If you say that a baby can't follow point 2, reproduce, then anyone who hasn't had puberty isn't a living thing. The fertilized egg evolves from one phase to another, going from a zygote to an embryo to a fetus. This is a small-scale, quick evolution, but it is still an evolution that has to do with growing and developing in utero.

In fact, the Pro-Life argument in the 1970s used modern science (at the time) to show how the fetus was a living thing, creating its own cells at birth and displaying pictures of the unborn children at different ages (1 week, 2 weeks, 3 weeks, etc.) and what happens at those ages. The court agreed to their proven statement of fetuses being alive.

Another statement made by my opponents is the fact that since I am not a female, my opinion is less qualified on the issue than that of a woman's. That's like saying that since I'm not a politician, I can't have a valid opinion about how the government should be run, or since I am not a slave owner, I don't get an opinion on slavery. Obviously, that is absurd and asinine in every way possible, but they still cling to this defense; how comical.

What's also comical is Judith Jarvis Thomson's argument on why abortion should be legal. He states that even if the fetus is a living human and has the rights to life, abortion should be morally acceptable because of the woman's right to control her body and its systems. The right to live is more important than a person's rights to reproduction and its faculties, especially when one used said faculties to have sex, which, if they get pregnant, they should accept the consequences of their actions.

In the trials preceding Roe v. Wade, one of the biggest opponents for Roe and Margie Pitts Hames (Hames was a Civil Rights Lawyer) was the Assistant State Attorney Dorothy Toth Beasley, a native to New Jersey that had moved down to Georgia and had worked at the same time as Hames. Beasley's central claim was that the United States Constitution doesn't give pregnant women the right to destroy a living child, the child was never a part of the mother because it was alive from the point of conception. Beasley says that the fetus "from its earliest stage already a boy or girl, with its own organs" and that the supposed right of abortion being argued in this trial (this case was Doe v. Bolton) had invaded the life and liberty of the unborn child; she is correct.

According to the people and scientists, for the first few weeks of pregnancy, which women don't know if they are pregnant until around week 3 or 4, it is just a ball of tissue. This is absurd. From the point of conception, the child is living; it's developing. By week 3, the baby is developing its nervous system; should it be able to be killed then? If so, then what about all of the paralyzed people? By week 4, it's developing its lungs; should it be killed then? What about all of the people on respiratory machines like the Iron Lungs? By week 22, the baby starts to create its own brainwaves; should we kill it before this point? What about all of the brain-dead people? Should we kill them, even though we know that they'll be fine if we wait a couple of weeks?

The Left on the political scale uses the statement of rape for why abortion should be legal; so let's get rid of all abortions except for abortions in the case of rape. They won't agree to this, or they already would have. They're exploiting an evil action that happens rarely to justify all abortions. That's like saying "Let's make all abortion illegal but abortion". I ask for a compromise, saying "Let's make all forms of abortion illegal except in the case of rape". They won't agree to these terms.

The Left also uses the case of their claims being morally right when talking about issues like Climate Change and the money gap between the rich and poor. They are literally killing the most innocent among us and just ignoring it; a critically asinine thing to do for anyone. The Left also claims that the people should not make claims and decisions based on emotion even though they do the same when talking about the Gun Control Debate.

The Pro-Choice side believes that all abortions ar whatever stage of pregnancy -- 1d trimester (when the child's heart is beating), 2d trimester (when the baby's brain is developed), and Third trimester (when the baby can live outside of the womb) -- and they justify it through rape and abortion "rightfully being the woman's choice" because it's in her body. A woman's body doesn't have two heads, four legs, four arms, two brains, and two hearts. Making the argument that since it's your body it's your choice is selfish and wrong. There was this terrible act in the United States's history that was a major factor in the split of the United States of America and the temporary Confederate States of America; it's called slavery. The Pro-Choice complain when a person who is Pro-Life uses slavery as an example. Slavery is related to this issue because it is both relatable to abortion and is a violation of human rights.

Abortion and Slavery are relatable because the claim for slavery to remain legal was because it took place on your private property, your Fifth Amendment, and because of the case of Dred Scott v. Sandford, which said that slaves were private property and could not be taken by the Government until the Thirteenth Amendment. The claim for abortion being that since it's insider her body (like how it's on the owner's land), it is her choice, and, coincidentally, they also have a United States Supreme Court Case backing them up called Roe v. Wade.

Abortion and Slavery are both violations of human rights. Regardless of government, we have negative rights, which are the rights that are current when a government is not present. The most famous of these are the three in the Trilogy "Life, Liberty, and the Pursuit of Happiness" in the Declaration of Independence. Abortion violates Life because you are killing a living, innocent being, and Slavery violates Liberty because you are holding someone somewhere they don't get a choice in, doing work that they are not willing to do.

All life starts at conception. Can it be single-celled? Yes. That's how N.A.S.A. would classify life on a foreign planet like Jupiter or Mars, so why should that change on Earth? From the moment of conception, a unique genealogy starts to happen. Undoubtedly, this is when life starts. All living things have cells, and every genealogical cell has chromosomes and DNA/RNA in it. This is where life starts. Trees have DNA/RNA. So does fish, and even the amoeba. All life has some form of genealogy in it (Universal Genetic Code), and that is unique to all life, and that is when life should be considered to start, including human life.

This is your warning: the next three paragraphs are descriptively graphic with gore. I suggest that if you have a light stomach to try to trek through it, but if you feel queasy, just stop reading, or you could have a friend read what the paragraphs say and then describe to you what happens in the abortion process, but keep in mind: I speak the truth.

What happens in the first-trimester abortion -- when the mother usually doesn't know that she is pregnant -- is that the developing child is sucked through a catheter, killing it. The Left calls this "terminating the pregnancy" or other euphemisms that mask the terrible truth of what abortion actually is: murder.

What happens with a second-trimester abortion -- the most common of abortions -- is that the child is too grown to just suck out as the doctors do in the first-trimester abortions, so what the doctors do after sucking the symbiotic fluid from around the infant out, is grab a special type of forceps called Sopher clamps that have teeth on the last two and a half inches with a width of around an inch, and are thirteen inches long, and they rip out the child limb by limb through the mother's vagina. The head is too large, so the doctors have to squeeze the head until a white substance leaks out of the vagina -- this is what would be the child's brain -- and then bring out the child's head, piece by piece, then the fluid is then sucked out of the womb by a catheter-like object.

What happens during a third-trimester abortion -- and this is just utterly immoral and cruel from every lens that you would view this from -- is that the baby, fully developed and can survive on its own, is pulled out of the mother's womb by the feet, except for the head, and takes a pointed steel instrument -- usually a pair of scissors -- and penetrate the baby's skull, then sticks a tube in the skull and sucks out the child's brain. If that were to happen outside of the womb -- and should be considered this inside the womb as well -- it would be considered first-degree murder. Sadly, third-trimester abortion is back on the rise with new laws being passed in New York stating that a legal abortion can happen until the moment of birth.

I do not hate the medical assassins for doing this, it's a part of their job (but I wouldn't call them a doctor due to purposely killing people), but what I hate is the people who get these done and the people who believe that it is their choice on whether the child, a living thing, lives or dies. The argument for abortion is a lot like the argument for slavery: if you are on my land, I get to choose if you are property or not; before the end of slavery, there were laws restricting slavery until the ratification of the Thirteenth Amendment. We should have another amendment to the U.S. Constitution that outlaws abortion, giving the negative/natural rights back to the unborn; after all, they aren't living under a government.

Some people will ask "What's your view on other birth control forms like sterilization or other forms of birth control other than abortion?" and I don't really care if you try to prevent a pregnancy because there is no life yet; however, when a woman is pregnant, the pregnancy is a separate life that should have their negative rights. Once again, I do not care if you get your ovary tubes tied, or if you use condoms, or if you get sterilized because that choice is yours to make, but when it affects another's life, then it is not entirely your choice to make: all of those birth control choices come before the pregnancy, when there is no life in question.

According to the Academic American Encyclopedia, 1980, abortion and other forms of pregnancy termination are also considered a form of birth control. Other than abortion, birth control forms are blocking off of the sperm and the egg by use of a barrier or withdrawal of the male's penis before ejaculation, and altering body functions by the use of drugs, usually for the women, but pharmacologists have recently developed an experimental drug for men to take that will supposedly prevent pregnancy, avoiding sex altogether, and getting sterilized.

I do not care if you use these alternate, true forms of birth control because they only affect your body, it is rightfully your choice, and there is no pregnancy, no life in question, no killing of the unborn. The only form of birth control that I have a problem with is abortion because there is a pregnancy, it is alive since conception, and it has its individual, nonnegotiable rights of living that shouldn't be taken away by the parents.

Why do I care if women have abortions or not? I care because I don't believe that we should play God and choose who lives and who dies. That is a human life; you don't get to kill it just because it's convenient that you do, nor do you get to kill it because of the claim that since it is in your body, you have total control of it. That baby is an individual and it has its rights, but they have been stripped away because your sense of convenience is so much mightier than the right of life to the purest of humans.

Even some Medical Doctors were against abortions primarily because it is infanticide. It is the legal killing of the unborn. In fact, Dr. Henry Gibbon made a statement that the abortionist audience had created "the serpent that tempts the woman to put to death their unborn offspring." Abortion is killing an unborn child: just because a child isn't born yet doesn't mean that it is not living. Modern science has proven that the unborn child is alive in *Roe v. Wade* and in modern science.

Religion is an important part and influence of this topic. Not everyone is of one religion, so I was trying to avoid using religion, but I've found a way to appeal to the majority of people. The previous paragraphs were designed to appeal to everyone, especially atheists. In the preceding paragraph, I am going to make a case to the Abrahamic Religions, which have the vast majority of the United States and the World.

In Judaism, the common belief is that life starts at conception, and after thirty days of being in the womb, life gets a soul; that's where the spirit starts in life. In Jewish law, it is accepted only to have an abortion if the life of the mother is in danger, like she is going to kill herself because of the pregnancy; in this issue, you have a complete soul -- the mother -- and an incomplete soul -- the unborn child -- and whenever you have to choose between the two, you choose the complete soul: the only exception in Judaism to have an abortion is with the life of the mother -- not her health, but her life.

In Christianity, the common belief is often like the one in Judaism, that it is bad for people to have abortions, and that abortion encourages infanticide. In fact, Vice President Pence did a good job describing why abortion is wrong religiously with citations and quotes from the Bible, mainly the Commandment "Thou Shalt Not Kill". Even the Catholics in the 1950s denounced Birth Control and Abortion because it promotes the idea that the purpose of having sex is to enjoy it and not necessarily to procreate, which makes Birth Control and Abortion unnatural processes.

In Islam, it pretty much is the same and can be seen as a disrespect to God/Allah, which is not taken lightly by the most strict Abrahamic religion.

In fact, it can be seen as a sin where you would have to redeem yourself during Ramadan, the Islamic Holy Month. In fact, in the Qur'an, the Islamic Holy Book, it says "do not kill your children for fear of poverty. It was We who provided (sic) for them as well as for you. Killing them is surely a grave sin!" (Qur'an, Al-Isra:31)

In the United States, the Senate has failed to pass a bill protecting infants that are born alive. Slowly and slowly, the Pro-Choice people have been criminalizing the right and moral stance of how abortion be illegal, even though they themselves (the Pro-Choice-ers) are backing up infanticide, the literal killing -- remember, we can't use murder because murder is illegal and unjust -- of infants and of the unborn.

We should obviously stop evil acts like killing people when we can. Murder is an illegal, horrific act that is rightfully made illegal. To a certain extent, murder is better than abortion (I use "better" as a lesser evil act) because infants are literally the most innocent of us humans. A fetus has never lied, stolen, killed, broken any laws, etc. They've also done nothing but exist, yet some people still feel the right to kill these innocent people.

Unborn children are still living and have their fundamental rights of Life and Liberty. Are we just going to let baby-killing happen, or are we going to give the rights of the unborn children back? They have the right to life, the same as us. When you claim that the Right to Choose is more important than the unborn's Right to Live, that's just selfish. You don't get to kill babies. If the mother is going to die from having a baby (from a lack of nutrition), then the baby could be seen as the murderer, and that is the only situation when abortion is acceptable: when the life of the mother is in threat of certain death from the fetus.

Finally, outlawing abortion isn't removing a woman's right to choose to have children or not: the woman chooses to have a kid or not when she has sex: being abstinent is a choice. What outlawing abortion does is allow the fetus to live and grow as a human.

On Gender

There has been major controversy on this topic. This chapter deals with Feminism, both modern and old, the L.G.B.T. Community, mainly the transgenders, but also brushing the homosexuals that are called bisexuals, lesbians, or gays. I've researched this topic grandly and immensely.

Feminism

Since the 1880s, there has been a movement of Feminism, the belief that both genders are equal and the rational act for women to gain the same rights as men -- necessary at the time. Since the year 2000 A.D.E., Feminism isn't needed; women had as many rights as men. What we needed State-sponsored Egalitarianism. Since 2000, Feminism took a turn for the worst, developing into a system that hates males and takes everything offensively, along with teaming up with the Social Justice Warriors in the early 2010s.

There are three phases or waves of Feminism. Firstly, being the basic egalitarian idea of men and women are equal and that women need to get their rights -- the basic idea that is not corrupt and is true in all logic -- which was around the late 1880s to the late 1910s, officially ending with national female suffrage (Wyoming was the first state where women could vote). Secondly, There is the second wave of Feminism that had happened between the 1920s to the 1950s with the Flappers and the idea that since women work now, they can do whatever a man can do -- which can get kind of annoying. Thirdly and finally, there is the third wave of Feminism from the 1970s to the present day that had the ridiculous claim that all men do something bad constantly like beat their wife and that the world is biased in the form of Masculine Superiority, but at that time in society, there was virtually no proof of that claim.

Modern Feminism can be seen in the book *The Feminine Mystique* by Betty Friedan, a Feminist, a Women's Rights leader and Pro-Choice activist whose main political fame happened in the 1960s. In *The Feminine Mystique*, Friedan makes the claim that women back in the 1960s haven't been treated as human because they live in a male-dominant society, which is completely wrong since, even at that time, women worked in jobs that men had previously worked for, women had their suffrage from the Nineteenth Amendment, and what she was promoting was illegal activities like marching on a street when the police officers told the marchers not to march on the street and to stay on the sidewalk and she also promoted women and doctors having illegal abortions just so that the doctors and women could get arrested, then tried to the State Supreme Court for the laws either to be reformed or removed entirely.

> "Saying that 'I've had three illegal abortions' aloud was my feminist baptism, my swift immersion in the power of sisterhood. A medical procedure I'd been forced to secure alone, shrouded in silence, was not 'a personal problem' any more than the matter of my gender in the newsroom [where she worked] was 'a personal problem.'"

Saying that you've had three illegal abortions is a right of passage to being a feminist? That's illegal and murder. Abortion is the legalized killing of the unborn child and the fact that it was illegal makes the Third-Wave Feminist Movement worse. They are willing to commit illegal acts against humanity just because they believe that they have the right to. If everything were like that -- that we'd have whatever rights just because we believed that we had them -- the public shooters wouldn't be criminals, the murderers wouldn't be arrested, there would be no crime because they feel like it would "be one of their rights".

In the *Feminine Mystique*, Friedan complains and attacks woman's choice to get married. She states:

> "By the end of the nineteen-fifties, the average marriage age of women dropped to 20, [sic] and was still dropping, [sic] into the teens. Fourteen million girls were engaged by 17. The proportion of women attending college in comparison with men dropped from 47 per cent [sic] in 1920 to 35 per cent [sic] in 1958. ... by the mid-fifties, 60 per cent [sic] dropped out of college to marry..."

It's a woman's choice to marry and to seek higher education, correct? So, if you're a feminist, then why are you attacking a women's choice when it is their education, their marriage, and their spirituality, but not when it's their body?

Men are men and women are women. The Left claims that women make about 77% of the men's salary, which is ridiculous. As early as 2010, the U.S.'s 50 biggest cities have more female workers than male workers, but they also take more time off than the men and work less dangerous jobs like being an electrician or a metal worker, all adding up to the lower amount of money that they are getting paid; I can guarantee you that if men were to do the same, the same result. It's not sexist in any way, it's just business, which is also why businesses appeal to the men more often than they do to the women. When women are asking for equal pay, they are asking for special treatment. There is already equality in the workplace between the two genders; there is fairness; the women just don't get paid as much as they want because they want to be with their families more than men do, and all the other reasons previously stated. When they ask for equal pay, they want their labor to be worth more just because they are a woman.

In fact, there is also the Equal Pay Act of 1963 which made a pay gap illegal. It was passed by President J.F.K., making equal pay for equal labor. There are still factors that are by choice that women also can do that contribute to this "gap". One of them is not joining the military. Women could have joined the military since the Twentieth Amendment because of Draft Laws at the time, which was later reformed to make it non-mandatory for registered voters to be signed up for the Draft. However, after World War Two, there was an act signed in 1948 allowing the integration of women into the Armed Forces, which also ended segregation in the Armed Forces. Being in the

Military is not only a dangerous job, but it is also a job that requires a lot of work, which is why the military members get pensions for their service.

Feminism is currently in a tangled spiral of idiocy; they aim for women to have an equal stance in society; they want women to be able to make their own decisions; however, when women make their choice and suffer the logical consequence of losing some pay, they revolt; they only follow their theories on society when it benefits them, not practicing what they preach. Pathetic (I am not calling women pathetic, but what the feminists are doing is sad, pathetic, and honestly embarrassing to our nation).

There is a "Believe Her" movement focusing on domestic violence. This movement is just lunacy! Statistically, men were charged more of domestic violence than women before this movement existed by a margin of up to forty to fifty percent, with men being accused in the sixty percent and women with only twelve percent accusations. This movement also encourages women to have the ability to just lie. The girl could just beat herself up with a hammer and then blame it on her spouse and the man will get charged with domestic violence falsely but the verdict will most likely be "guilty".

Often, feminists when a man holds open a door for them; they believe that it shows the suppression of women and misogynistic rule. I can tell you that they hold open the doors for human decency. Most people are egalitarian -- the idea and movement of both genders being equal and treated equally. It is the group that hasn't gone astray from the path of righteousness; they are a group of people that believe in equality between the two genders; they have human decency and are criticized for having morals: what a shame we humans have become.

Sometimes, there are logical feminists that believe in the old Feminism from back in the early 1900s. I know of a teacher that can't tell me if they (I use "they" in order to save identity) are a feminist, but I know that they are. They are a logical feminist; they abide and practices what they preach, following their theories when they don't benefit themselves. If you are a logical feminist like that teacher, then nearly nothing of these past paragraphs apply to you, but they still, however, should make you think about how the modern Feminism is twisted, and how a return is needed.

As for the movement of including boys and girls from the time of being a child (5 - 10 years) to their teens, I have no problem with it, so long as they do such gender-neutral activities like a book club or language clubs. Not, however, should women be able to join a club exclusively for men, nor should men be able to join clubs exclusively for women. Back in the mid-2010s, young ladies wanted to join the Boy Scouts of America, but they were denied, which led to an extreme and critical part of our history. Eventually, the Boy Scouts of America had changed their name to the Scouts of America and their policy to allow women to join. This wouldn't be such a problem if the Girl Scouts of America had either merged with the new Scouts of America or had disbanded, but they did neither. Here's a challenge to them; let's have biological men try to join, just for them to be rejected, and then do what the women had done to the Boy Scouts of America. Honestly, why don't we? After all, the ideology of Feminism is to make women have the same rights as men. They won't do so, however, because Feminism has been changed over time so drastically that it will only be used in someone's defense, allowing them to decline the effects that their actions caused.

The term "sexism" or "sexist" itself is sexist. It is when something positive is applied only to men or when something negative is only applied to women. It is stated that men using profanity are sexist to women. "Sexist" should apply to policies that should not differ between the two genders but does anyway. That is what the proper term should be.

If women were to beat a man, it would not get covered in the media or the news. I have never heard of a domestic violence case where the woman beats the man and she is punished in the news media. People will claim that it doesn't happen, which is just garbage; I know that this happens: I've seen it unravel myself. If women want equal rights, they should be able to be charged with domestic abuse and domestic violence without prejudice.

There is a specter haunting America -- the specter of Toxic Masculinity. This term is one that is used to define when men do something terrible like a fight. This is not from too much masculinity but from a lack of. The generation that has had a miss of a father-figure, a positive influence of masculinity, not showing this generation what to do and how to handle their emotions.

Here's a question for the modern Feminists: why don't you fight for the rights of the oppressed women in Muslim communities and countries like Pakistan, Egypt, Iraq, Saudi Arabia, etc.? Why don't you? Because it's the woman's choice to exercise her First Amendment Right under its Practice clause to be lesser than men? Women in the United States have these choices, not only for religion. Take a look at the Fourteenth Amendment, which is EQUALITY under the Law.

Final point to make on Feminism: the right to vote was given to the people who signed up for the Draft, willing to die for their country. If you don't sign up for the Draft, you shouldn't be able to vote. I know men and women are different, and that is why I suggest a separate Draft for women, being mandatory nurse service in an emergency.

L.G.B.T. Community/Transgenders

These next few paragraphs are going to make a select group of people angry. That select group is the L.G.B.T. community, so take this as your trigger warning. The irrational claim that there are more than two genders and that genders are based on emotions and an individual's personal estrogen and testosterone levels are just that -- irrational. Does anyone else see how ridiculous this is? Gender is dictated by what set of genitalia you were born with: if you were born with a penis, you are a biological male; if you were born with a vagina, then you are a biological female.

What a transgender person is, is a person with Gender Dysphoria, claiming membership to the gender of which they are not apart of. They are still people, just people with a mental disorder. As stated before, if you were born with a penis that didn't change into a vagina naturally, you are a male. The same is true for females and vaginas. The answer to the question "What to do to treat Gender Dysphoria" is not to allow them to dictate what we call them, but to call them by what they are.

It is suggested that since the suicide rate of transgenders is at an alarming high percent -- 40 percent -- bullying plays a major factor. If that were true, then the transgenders must be experiencing the same type of treatment experienced by the European Jews during the years from 1934 to 1945. The idea that bullying is the main factor (I am not stating that bullying isn't a factor, just that it is not the main factor) behind the suicide rate is asinine and a jackass claim. The suicide rate is so high because they are experiencing a mental disorder. There has to be some sort of correct treatment for it, but it won't be us, the mentally sane, compromising our 1d amendment rights and calling them something that they aren't, that is not an opinion. Ben Shapiro has a great motto which is "Facts don't care about your feelings" (even though he is a hypocrite about his own motto) and that is completely true in all issues -- including this one. If we were to use the treatment suggested by the mentally ill, that would be like going up to a person with Paranoid Schizophrenia and agreeing with them that Uncle Sam is out to get them. That's not the proper treatment.

The proof that the sex-reassignment surgery doesn't work is that the suicide rate is about the same percentage as before the surgery. There are people who encourage transgenderism in children. How more idiotic can you get? Children don't know what they really are until puberty hits when they are teenagers. Children can't be transgender; once puberty hits, they know what they are and that is that. The claim that they feel like something else is also complete insanity. If you've never been that thing, then how do you know how they feel? It's like being trans-species. If I were to use their claim, then I'd say that "I feel like a dog, so you must call me a dog." I am a human. I cannot change my gender, race, age, or species.

Gender and sex aren't disconnected, nor should they be. Gender is supposedly a social structure -- even though if your gender doesn't match your sex you have a legitimate mental illness called Gender Dysphoria -- and sex is what you actually are. If you have a mental issue because your gender is different than your sex, then sex and gender aren't disconnected at all! Supposedly, we do not know what truly defines a person's gender, even though we have a great system that studies life called Biology; in this scientific field, there is a study of genetics in life that affect your height, weight, eye color, and even your risk for diseases: this scientific field in Biology is called Chromosomal Biology.

In Chromosomal Biology, the gene in the chromosomes -- the parts that make the DNA of an individual -- that define a person's gender has two parts labeled an "X" gene and a "Y" gene. In the chromosome that determines a person's gender, it contains two genes. Everyone has at least one X gene in each of their cells. The X gene makes females. The Y genes make the males. Every biological male has both an X and Y gene and every biological female has two X genes. You are BORN with these genes. When your cells repair themselves by creating new cells, those new cells have the SAME genes as the cells before them. It is IMPOSSIBLE to change your sex. I cannot stress this enough.

Even if you have sex disorders where you are either missing a sex defining chromosome, you have a gender. Genitalia is primary sex definers and other characteristics like breasts, hips, and amount of hair are all secondary sex definers. If you have a male's set of genitalia and a set of breasts from a disease caused by an extra X chromosome, then you are a male with a genetic disease. You should have surgery to remove the breasts.

People cannot change their gender. There's the psychological factor: men are usually more into action and women are more into princesses for the most part. (I speak from experience. I am a male who has one brother and two sisters.) Men and women can still like the contrary, but it still doesn't change someone's gender, and neither does sex reassignment surgery, nor both together. If you are a woman who likes trucks and action, then you're a butch, man-like woman (which isn't a wrong thing to be). The same is true for a flower-gardening, emotional, woman-like man, you're just a feminine man (which still isn't wrong). Regardless of if you are Feminine or Masculine, you are still either a born, biological woman or man and that does not change.

Once again, those whose prefered gender differs from their biological sex have this mental illness formerly called Gender Identity Disease, currently called Gender Dysphoria, which is linked to depression and suicide, not from the famed "bullying" factor (there was acceptance since the early 2010s and the rate of suicide remained the same) but because of their mental illness.

Now, the L.G.B.T. Community is trying to say that you cannot assume someone's gender based on their physical appearance, which is exceedingly falsified. There are primary and secondary gender characteristics that we can use, at first sight, to assume what their gender is. As stated, there are characteristics designated to each gender of people. If I were to describe to you someone with short hair, who wears hoodies and straight, bootcut jeans, then you are right to automatically assume that the person I described is a male (if you can't tell their body shape or see their face (men and women have different bone structures)); if I were to describe a person with long hair, tight pants, and a smaller shirt (crop tops, stomach shirts, etc.), then you'd be correct in assuming that the person is a female (under the same conditions previously described). Now, people don't have to wear those specific articles of clothing, but those were examples and are usually worn by those genders, but a man can have long hair and wear tight pants, but they decide to accept judgment every morning when they get dressed in the morning.

First, there are primary and Secondary gender-determining characteristics. The primary characteristics are parts of genitalia like the penis and vagina. The penis is a male organ, and so are the sperm ducts, the testes, and the scrotum, along with the XY chromosome pair. The vagina is a female organ, and so is the womb, ovaries, fallopian tubes, the XX chromosome pair, etc. Biology, in short, is the Primary gender-defining characteristics. *Second*, there are secondary gender-defining characteristics that consist of hair length, the clothes that you wear, etc. In short, characteristics that are defined by either us or appear after puberty, such as hair length, the clothes that you wear, and, surprisingly, breasts as well (men can have breasts if their body fat is high enough).

There are the Intersex individuals (who used to be called Hermaphrodites as a medical term because they have one gender's primary sex characteristics and the other's secondary sex characteristics). These diseases are Klinefelter's Syndrome, CAH, AIS, etc. These diseases all either have male sex characteristics or female sex characteristics. They are not excuses to the transgenders; the intersex are either men or women, not both, but one or the other and they will remain that one for so long as they live.

If no primary characteristics are present, then you can use the secondary characteristics to assume someone's gender, but if they say that you're wrong and show you primary characteristics that counteract the secondary characteristics, the primary characteristics prevail. For instance, if I see a person in a metro who is wearing a dress and has long hair, I could call them "miss" and I'd be correct; however, if they were to turn around and say "sorry, I'm a male" and they show me their primary characteristics, then I was wrong. It is as simple as that.

Instead of just allowing people to assume a person's gender based on their characteristics, they make up fake pronouns to use in speech when talking about them. Men and women are different inherently, which is why there are two genders. The idea of gender fluidity is just futile and wrong: there might as well be one universal gender for all species of life. If you want to be called "her" and you are a male, I won't call you by what you want to be called, I'll call you by what you are. The same for someone wanting to be called "it" or "they" or even "ze". Pure idiocy had created this.

Another part of the L.G.B.T. Community is the idea that bisexuality and homosexuality should be allowed and accepted in society. I have no problem with these people who go against nature and could possibly have a mental disorder unless they try making the claim for something that is untrue and wrong like if they use the claim that two biological men can create a child themselves. I don't have a problem with the bis and the gays, even if they aren't natural and go against nature because they aren't wrong on their claims. (They do not claim to be able to reproduce with the same gender.)

For the other parts of the L.G.B.T. Community (the homosexuals and bisexuals), I do not believe that they all have some sort of mental illness, unlike all transgenders. From my knowledge, the bisexuals don't really care for the gender of their partner, which is just not caring and not a mental disorder.

There are two types of homosexuals: those by choice and those by nature. Those by choice are making a decision that I would not recommend to anyone and will probably face discrimination for it, but we all do for our choices; however, they don't have any apparent mental illnesses because it is by choice.

The other type of homosexuals, the ones by nature, may have a mental illness because it is not natural for someone to be attracted to the same sex. The term for the mental illness that causes natural homosexuality I will be calling "homophilia". This would be a minor mental illness easy to live with and not dangerous, so it is a little like Autism in the way that they are both minor mental illnesses. Treatment for homophilia would have to happen during childhood or adolescence because those are the years that the children are the most impressionable. Homophilia isn't illegal in any way, so no federal or national action is needed. Also, the homophiles make no claim against nature itself and biology (unlike the transgenders) so we do not need to bother them, so long as they stay peaceful, lawful, and correct.

As for the L.G.B.T. community itself, they just want people to be whatever makes them happy, no matter how absurd. They support the idea that boys can be girls and girls being boys, and the idea that a 60-year-old can become a 14-year-old, and many other ridiculous, wanton ideas. Just because you think you are something that doesn't make you that thing. I may believe that I am an Apache Helicopter, but am I? No. The L.G.B.T. community has lost touch with reality and so has all of its supporters. There are some parts of life that we can't change and should be respected, like gender, race, and age. None of those are malleable -- except for age; that changes over time -- and anyone who thinks that way is delusional.

On Family

By Western Culture or possibly worldwide, Family consists of anyone who lives in your household (Father, Mother, Children, possible grandparents, etc.) and the roles that they play. It is seen that the children are still forming and don't have their rights and their opinions don't matter, the mother is to take care and raise the children, and that the Father is to provide for the family. This is generalized: of course, there can be single parents who provide for their family.

The idea that children don't have their natural rights pointed out in Common Sense by Thomas Paine -- which is in the Declaration of Independence -- nor their rights to governmental rights like suffrage. The natural rights that people should have without a government are Life, Liberty, and the Pursuit of Happiness, and if the government does not protect those rights of the citizens, then it should be abolished. The unnatural rights, the rights that are given to the people during a government, are additional, but should not interfere with the fundamental, natural rights of man. In the U.S.A., we have the amendments of the United States that define what rights that the individual has --usually in the Bill of Rights. These rights apply to the citizens, and should no matter what age for the harmless ones like the First Amendment, but not for the Second Amendment.

In the previous paragraph, it is stated that the idea of children not having their natural rights is controversial. Do I believe that children, no matter their age, should receive their natural rights? Of course, I do, which, in reflect, can also be proven by my stances on other controversial issues like abortion. The three parts of natural rights are Life, Liberty and the pursuit of happiness.

Firstly, everyone has the right to live. No-one should be able to "Sentence someone to the Stone". Do I believe that crimes should be met with punishment? Yes, but I also believe that the criminals have the right to live as well: that's why I believe that convicted rapers should be castrated instead of killed, but that's up to the State to decide.

Secondly, everyone has the right to Liberty. What is the right to Liberty? The right to Liberty is the right to be free because it is the nature of living things to be free. Humans aren't supposed to reign over one another, but they are also social creatures like primates, who use brute force and display in a lust for power and control. We ended Slavery for Family and Liberty.

Finally, everyone has the right to go in search of and be happy. If pets make you happy, have pets. If polygamy makes you happy, be a polygamist. The trick with this natural right is that it can not cross the rights of others. Staying with the Polygamy example, since the spouse has the right to Liberty, it should be a consensual agreement for marriage and all terms to it.

I believe that every human should have these three natural rights, no matter what your age, social status, race, religion, family status, etc.

In Family, the role of the Father (sometimes also taken as a role of the mother as well) is to provide for his children and others in the household. This is protecting the members of the household in a community, helping them to survive. They are the sheepdog for the chickens against the fox. This role can be taken up by the other parent, the mother, or by other people like guardians. This is obviously a highly important role in the Family.

The role of the Mother in Family is to provide and protect the children. From birth, the Mother is the one person that the child should always be able to trust. It is natural for women after childbirth to nurse the child and help them. No matter what Cathy Areu says, breastfeeding is a natural process that only happens to women for a select period of time after childbirth. My statements aren't sexist in any way: often, women like to be with infants and young children; It is not sexist for me to state a fact, and that fact is that the role of the Mother in Family is to provide for the children. Both parental roles are fundamental to the family.

It has become accepted since World War One that women and mothers should work for money and help provide for their families as well as their infant children. As children develop, however, it is apparent and natural for women to take less and less care of that child as they are less dependent, and/or if the mother has another child younger than the first. This is completely acceptable.

If in a family, there is only one parent, then the remaining parent, father or mother, would usually rise to the challenge and try to do the job of both parents. Most of the time, they will fail by the slightest amount because the child won't have them as a heroin or masculine role model to model themselves after and to look up to. (This is a cause of Toxic Masculinity and anger issues in the youth.)

As previously stated, it is seen that since children are still forming, their opinions do not matter and that they should not have rights and that is because often, children have different opinions than their parents and they -- the parents -- shut up their children so that they don't have to hear any of their opinions -- a fascist act to silence opposing political views. If I were a parent, I would not silence my children, rather then show them why they are wrong in their opinions -- which can be possible. Children, too, should have rights because of the Fourteenth Amendment of anyone born on U.S. soil being a citizen and the case of *Engel v. Vitale*.

There is apparently a plague of "toxic masculinity" among the new generation and the new adults. Some people claim it to be masculinity in its pure form, but they are wrong. What happened to create this toxic masculinity is that there was a huge spike from the percent of people who left their families; since this happened about a decade ago, the new generation, especially the males, has no person as a role model on how to be in society and how to control their feelings; this is why the domestic violence rate is so high. What Feminists are trying to do is make masculinity seem naturally terrible and that it should be restricted: isn't that a sexist thing to do? They wouldn't say so because it doesn't attack women.

Particularly fathers leave the family in order to try to make their lives better by working more. This is because of the higher tax rate and the natural sense of greed among people. What society needs in the Family issue and question is a return to normalcy. We should force this next generation to be with their families in a financial way. They will coincide with financial pressure and hopefully, everything will be back to normal, like the Family model in the '60s and '70s of the last century.

In this aspect of society, sadly, we also need a return to normalcy, but with some minor changes in women's rights, male discrimination, and child rights. Women should be able to work and have as many rights as men, along with having as valid an opinion as men; men shouldn't feel like they have to leave to get more money and better their lives; children should not be discriminated against because of their age and neither should some certain, non harmful rights, nor their political opinions, given that they can back up their position.

So how can we help fix these problems? The quick answer is we cannot do so reasonably. I am not for Social Security, and you shouldn't be either, but we cannot force a company to give unqualified people jobs. It's sink or swim. But, if there were more companies, there would be more jobs to fill, potentially allowing for those less-qualified people to obtain jobs and be trained, becoming more qualified for the job they applied to and future jobs, which also helps the economy out in the process due to a new business and more people spending money, along with creating a better role model for the kids than a jobless loather.

On Government

There are many types of governments; a few being Monarchy, Democracy, Empire, Dictatorship, Republic, Dynasty, Despotism, and One-party leadership. There are many types of each, with democracy having, no doubtfully, the most variant ways than the others. If you look through history and the Earth, then you will see that Democracy has taken a strong foothold and the Empires and Monarchies of old have vanished. This is because people want a voice in how the complexities of government are being run in their society.

Despotism is one of, if not the oldest, forms of government. It is when a sole-ruler does whatever he or she desires wantonly. The best example of this that I can find of this is Xerxes of the Persian Empire; he had issued his engineers to construct a bridge made of boats. When the bridge failed, he executed the engineers and sent for a new crew to try the same feat. Luckily, they succeeded.

Monarchy is one of the most classical, popular, and medieval governments. In a Monarchy, close to Imperial, there is a King, the Royal Family, and the Nobles. The Nobles, also for Imperial, has ranks of social hierarchy like Viscount, Knight, Bishop, etc.

There are three types of monarchy: Absolute, Constitutional, and Figurehead. Firstly, the Absolute Monarchy is like a Dictatorship; the leader of the Royal Family has complete control over the people and government -- the best example is of Great Britain before their Civil War that had created the Magna Charta.

Secondly, a Constitutional Monarchy has the leader of the Royal Family in charge of the Government, but its power is limited to a constitutional document, like the Magna Charta. The Constitutional Monarchy is more democratic than the Absolute Monarchy, and it is more of a compromise between the Ruler and the Peasants.

Finally, a Figurehead Monarchy is when the head of the Royal Family has no more power than the average citizen of the kingdom or area. Of course, this idea is not too popular among people because people are naturally greedy for power. Since people are greedy, I have no good example of this type of Monarchy, but a quasi-example is the Ancient Hawaiian Kingdom before European intervened.

Monarchy is not as much of a successful government system as people uneducated on the subject would think. Most Monarchies lasted only a couple of generations peacefully until there was a killing of the head of the Royal Family. The most famous Monarchy is that of Saudi Arabia and its Royal Family. The more successful cousin of Monarchy is the Empire, which is up next.

Imperial is the system of Government used by Empires, like the French with Napoleon Bonaparte, the Roman with the Caesars, the German with their Kaisers, and the Chinese with their Dynastical Emperorship. Imperial is like the Constitutional Monarchy in some aspects but is also not like it in some aspects. The Emperor can be forced to back down from actions, unlike Monarchy, but the leadership of the Emperor also follows the Royal Family, but it is massively expanded to include nieces, nephews, uncles, all within the Noble standards of Dukes, Dutchesses, Viscounts, Knights, etc.

The Republic is the government that follows the theory of Republicanism. The theory of Republicanism is the theory of a representative government. Originally, until Pompey the Great, Rome was an equal Republic, having unelected representatives from a set area of the Empire all be in a council. Currently, we U.S. citizens live in the

Democratic Republic where we have elected representatives in the Federal Government and State Government.

A Dictatorship is when a single person, usually a military official, has complete control over the government. Dictatorships can also tie into One-party leadership, Absolute Monarchy, Dynasty, and Imperial. Some of the most famous dictatorships are Adolf Hitler and Nazi Germany, Benito Mussolini and Fascist Italy, Joseph Stalin and the U.S.S.R., Fidel Castro and Communist Cuba, North Korea, Mao Zedong, and Communist China, China's Dynasties, etc. Dictatorships are also called autocracies because autocracies are a form of a dictatorship. Autocracies do not need a leader to be a part of the military and use that as a force, rather a political force. Despite claims from the Economist, Russia is a Democratic Federation and not an Autocracy.

A Dynasty is like a Monarchy, but is more Asian -- and that is not a racist term, almost all Dynasties are Asian. The son of the Emperor would take the throne when his father dies, and the Emperor usually never gives up their power until death -- kind of like the Catholic Popes. During Ancient China's days, there were many different

Dynasties, all with their own Emperors, one of the most famous being the Wu Dynasty.

One-Party Leadership is when there is only one political party in the country and it controls the government; all other political parties are made illegal and the members will be arrested for. Famous One-party Leaderships are Fascist Italy, Nazi Germany, Communist Cuba, Vietnam, Korea, and Cameroon.

A Democratic Government is the most common one found in the world currently. The most common form of democracy is a republic, but there are also Confederacies and Federations. Republics have already been stated, but democratically, the representatives are elected, usually in terms. The United States of America and most European countries are the best examples of the Democratic Republic.

Confederacies have the weakest Federal Government and the least amount of centralization. The Confederate States of America, which had only lasted between 1859 to 1866 (due to the American Civil War), the U.S.S.R., and the U.S. under the Articles of Confederation are the best examples of the Democratic Confederation. I am actually most in favor of a Confederation because the individualized power of the state over the Federal Government. It makes us think more as a state and a local community than as a federal government, removing government from the people's lives more than when compared to Republics.

Federations have the strongest form of Centralization of power, and their leaders are elected as well. Usually, Federations do not have the electoral college that other Democracies have. The Russian Federation and the Federation of Germany are good examples of the Democratic Federation.

On the other extreme, there is Fascism, a political ideology that is now used as a slur in today's political age. The origins of Fascism come from Italy with the Italian word "fascismo", which sparked the idea of the collective being more important than the individual. This is just pluralism in its purest form, but fascism was morphed into a dictatorship during the 1920s after World War One in the ruins of Europe with its start in Italy with its leader Benito Mussolini, and how it spread to Adolf Hitler in Nazi Germany, and Franco in Spain. The Modern version of Fascism (the one inspired by Mussolini) is a forced form of Capitalism in a market controlled by the authoritarian/totalitarian State.

There is also another political system on the rise and is relatively recently created. It was designed in the 1850s by Karl Marx but was first put into practice by Vladimir I. Lenin and then further corruption happened with Joseph Stalin and Mao Zedong. What socialism is supposed to be is a strong State government without capitalism. The workers work directly for the state and the state gives them food, shelter, and clothing. Not a good ideology to have. No food, no God, no land.

You already know I favor a Confederacy because of the removal of Government from every-day life. Remove the government from people's lives and maybe God will be let back in.

On Economy

The economy is the blood of any country, and the people act as veins, and government, the bone. Just like anybody, you need to have a good source of blood. To do that, we need to have a stable, strong economy. Without that, your country would be sickly and weak. The United States during the Great Depression had such a terrible GDP of $66 billion per year and economy that the only thing that would fix the depression was war.

Basic Economics

Economics has been around since humans started trading in communities instead of just stealing the commodity and/or killing the owner. The most successful style of economics is capitalism, leading to the prosperity of nations and of people in general. There are those who would argue and attack capitalism, mainly the marxists and the socialists who own the institutions of which they complain about. I am qualified to talk about the benefits of capitalism versus the burdens of socialism not because of a degree that hangs on a wall, but because of logic that caused me to turn from socialism to capitalism.

Many of this section of the book is going to be similar to what Thomas Sowell says in his books, mainly basic economics. Of course, since capitalism has been around for longer than the Catholic Church, none of this is an original idea.

First, there's the combat between supply and demand. This is a pretty simple idea, doesn't take a degree or anything to understand. It is, in essence, the supply of a product must meet the demand of the same product in society. Not anything too large. The supply is the harder of the two to change. If you need more, you buy more, but to do that, you're already investing your own money, for instance, when you could change the demand of the item and make more equity that way.

For instance, say I was selling coats. I could sell coats at $30,000 per 1,000 units and I could only produce 1,000 units per month. These are really nice coats, it takes $10 to make a coat ($10,000 per 1,000 coats). If the demand for the coats, at, let's say, the Burlington Coat Factory rose above 1,000 per month, instead of buying another factory to produce more coats, I could raise the cost of the coats to $33,000 per 1,000 units, decreasing the demand because less people will either be able or willing to put the coat at that price. I would still be making more money, and investing the same amount of money, creating a larger margin of profit.

Now, since these coats aren't designer coats, I couldn't raise the price to around $100,000 per 1,000 units if the demand rises more because it wouldn't be worth it. Then, I would invest in another factory to produce the coats. If the opposite happens, then vice versa.

The enemy to the common man is inflation. It makes the money that you have stored away, in your jars, boxes, etc, worth less. Anyone would have a problem with this except the government and the tax collectors because they could better collect taxes from the citizens. A great way to combat inflation is with employment of citizens in companies. Sadly, this doesn't necessarily stop the Fed from creating more money from the mint presses, but it can influence their decision to do so. That's another reason why big business is a good thing, both to the common man and the wealthy owner.

Now, socialism is a different concept than the free market and almost any market you might see if you grew up in the Western world, bar some. The main idea behind socialism is from Karl Marx and the phrase "from each according to his ability to each according to his need". This means 'you work all you can and only take what you need'. This would create a giant surplus, economically lethal for any business, but looking at it morally, it's a good idea. The flaw in it is the force of it. It's not a charity when people come into your house and take your stuff that you earned. Giving to charity is a virtue that we all can enjoy, but socialism is not charity.

Economy ties into Government. Not just the GOP, or the Dems, but the fundamental type of government itself. In the United States, we have a Representative Republic where the Federal District (Washington D.C.) is funded by all citizens, but the States are funded by their own citizens, so, odds are, the state government is taxing you more than the Federal Government. This system works because of Federalism and the unity between separate nations (the States) who form a government that affects all of them, making them united. It is more important for a citizen to view themselves as a member of their local community before one of their state, and one of their state than one of their country. It is out of personal interest, but doesn't mean we shouldn't pay attention at the national level, just not as much as most people do now. This is mainly from the large journalism companies like Fox, CNN, NBS, ABC, etc. because they are a nation-wid business, not a state-wide business.

A fundamentalist government is proven to make their citizens the happiest, but it is also a religious government with High Priests and Priestesses as their leaders, so I guess you could say that it's like the Israelite people before King Saul with Moses, Aaron, Eliezer, etc. I am partial to this type of government (I am a Theocratic Monarchist), but back to the point. The government would be run by the Church, making taxes imposed to help the Church, removing the sacred virtue of charity. That is the only flaw to this system. You could have eternal life, not go to Hell, but be forced to pay for the church. Thanks to the Second Vatican Council, it is addressed that the Church and the State should be separate entities for this reason of Free Will. Regardless, I am still for a Monarchy with God as King.

Self-dependency should be a goal for any nation. Sadly, not all countries could become self-dependent, but that's what the global market is for. Decreasing the deficit (negative amount between the demand and the supply) helps nations become more wealthy until businesses can build more factories and become self-dependent, and then can sell their surplus on the global market. Now, the global market isn't as important as the local market for the same reason as before with the local community being more important than the federal government.

A country's import value should not exceed the country's export value because then the country is losing its money and its worth. An example is that the United State's debt from 2008 has risen from eleven trillion to twenty-one trillion in one decade because the U.S. is purchasing more from countries like China, India, Taiwan, Vietnam, etc. then they are selling their products like medicine, weapons, lumber, etc (kind of involves Joe Biden outsourcing our factories to China).

A Free Market entails the private businesses not being subject to the government on terms of what to sell. Many people are against monopolies because they see it as an anti-Free Market because the big guys versus the small guys, which I understand. What they don't realize is the small guys flourish in small towns where the big guys aren't and probably won't be for at least the next 100 years.

There were many monopolies in the United States during the late 1800s, mainly in oil and railroad. These companies did a great job producing what they promised, whether it be oil, railroad, or steel. It's good for those companies to have that large of a share in the market because they earned it. The same is for a new competitor in a market. If they create some sort of innovation, they deserve the market share they get. Innovations are protected by patons, anyways.

Many people dislike having monopolies, yet enjoy some aspects of monopolies. Exxon Mobil, for example, is an oil company, and their oil is reported to increase the lifespan of your car's engine. For an innovation such as that, they deserve their share in the market. Another reason why people dislike monopolies (and this is coming from Marxist theory) is because they believe the companies will try to streign the most amount of money from the people that they can. This is false. If the companies depend on how much money you have to buy their product, they wouldn't increase the price of their product to the point where you can barely purchase their goods. That's not financially sane to do in the case of a depression, for example.

Taxes

In monarchies, it was required to pay a heavy tax almost always, and when there was a war

-- which often was in Europe (unless you count the area of time between the 1300s and the 1600s), usually between France and England. During the Napoleonic War, the high taxes changed. In his Civil Code, Napoleon established a new measurement system called the Metric system that is more superior to and would replace the old Imperial system. Through Napoleon's reign, the countries that were allied with him (Naples, Switzerland, Spain, the Ottoman Empire, etc.) had begun to use his system more often until it was their primary system. In 1812, Napoleon retreating from a quasi-failed invasion into Russia, Napoleon was starting to lose. He lost his war, but his legacy of the Metric system lived on, which, bringing us back to our topic, had allowed Napoleon to tax his citizens more efficiently, allowing him to fight against the richest country at the time, England, for half a decade.

In democracies, the tax rates are chosen by the former and the people have to listen to it or be arrested. Through republicanism, we people have a little say through our elected officials. Regardless, if the representative doesn't do as we say, then the odds are that when an election comes back, they won't continue being our representative. That's the beauty of republicanism: we people actually have a say in our government. In fact, republicanism was one of the first steps for England's democracy with the Magna Charta. Undeniably, republicanism is an important step to both the government and the economy.

There is this thing called the Free Market that states you can choose what you buy and sell. Capitalism thrives on this market theory because there are more businesses, buying and selling commodities. For international shipping on products, however, the government has a say on tariffs (just think of them as taxes on products that regulate the supply and demand). That's completely understandable since the company and its product was made in the exporting country.

I agree that we need a Free Market because It is the best economic, free system that allows for prosperous growth of the economy, industry, and nation. Countries economically thrive when they have a Free Market, but I believe that we need a true Free Market where a company can own the entire percentage of the commodity field (relatively when talking about the large cities and not the small villages).

Governments make their money by taxing its citizens, usually small percent for both land and average income. Metropolitan areas like Los

Angeles, California, make a lot more money than rural villages like East Jordan, Michigan, but require more maintenance due to the higher population. When you tax the citizens in the cities who make a higher amount of money at a higher percent, then a lot of the citizens will move out of the city, which forces you to tax the remaining citizens of those metropolitan areas at a higher rate, ruining the economic proficiency of that area.

Currently in the United States, Representative Alexandria Ocasio-Cortez of New York has recommended a tax reform plan with a rate of seventy percent to ninety percent on the super-wealthy like Jeff Bezos, Bill Gates, etc. in her "Green New Deal" that also calls for a ban on airplane travels, restricted fossil fuel use, and other subjects like dealing with unemployment and poverty. If we tax the businesses too much, we will drive out business and money, hurting the American economy drastically (see Paragraph 2, Subsection H, i-iii of the Green New Deal).

Like in the days of the "Wild West", we shouldn't trust a cure-all without reason. For instance, how would we, the United States mainland, reach our state of Hawaii? By boat, which would use more fossil fuels than flying an airplane, or by building an underwater railway, which would take close to a decade to complete? Planes are more efficient than the recommended traveling, which is trains.

What she also forgets is that the United States is not a major world polluter, unlike China and India. Regardless of if we make these cutbacks, India and China will still pollute unless we help them in some way, preferably by annual loans for eco-friendly factories and India and China can pay back the loan with interest from the profits of these newly built factories.

What we can do for a tax rate is create a flat tax rate from the amount of land owned and the amount of income made annually (keep in mind this is at the Federal level, I am not going to address the State level). Right now, in early 2019 (taxes aren't due right now so no tax rate is issued. I am using the 2018 tax rate.), the lowest tax rate was 10 percent for an individual who makes up to $9,525 and the same rate but $19,050 for married people filing jointly. The highest rate was 37% for individuals who made $500,000 or more a year and 37% for married people who file jointly who make $600,000 or over annually.

What I suggest is a flat rate of 5-10% of one's fiscal year when all their assets are calculated together. This encourages business and is a tax because of citizenship, not because of wealth.

Bibliography

Articles

"2018 Poverty Guidelines." *ASPE*, 11 Jan. 2019, aspe.hhs.gov/2018-poverty-guidelines.

"Abortion Debate." *Wikipedia*, Wikimedia Foundation, 2 Mar. 2019, en.wikipedia.org/wiki/Abortion_debate.

"Abortion Statistics in the United States." *Wikipedia*, Wikimedia Foundation, 28 Feb. 2019,
en.wikipedia.org/wiki/Abortion_statistics_in_the_United_States.

Berger, Rob. "The New 2018 Federal Income Tax Bracket." *Forbes*, Forbes, 2017, www.forbes.com/sites/robertberger/2017/12/17/the-new-2018-federal-income-tax-brackets-rates/#4de1e8f7292a.

Editors, History.com. "Civil Rights Act of 1964." *History.com*, A&E Television Networks, 4 Jan. 2010, www.history.com/topics/black-history/civil-rights-act.

Finer, Lawrence B., and Mia R. Zolna. "Unintended Pregnancy in the United States: Incidence and Disparities, 2006." *National Center for Biotechnology Information*, 2011, www.ncbi.nlm.nih.gov/pmc/articles/PMC33 38192/.

"Highlights in the History of Military Women." *Timeline*, The Women's Memorial, www.womensmemorial.org/timeline.

Lee, Mike. "Lee Introduces Pain-Capable Abortion Restriction in DC." *Protecting the First Amendment*, www.lee.senate.gov/public/index.cfm/2012/ 2/lee-introduces-pain-capable-abortion-restri ction-in-dc.

"Marshall University." *Womens Center*, www.marshall.edu/wcenter/sexual-assault/ra pe-culture/.

"Pro-Life This Week - March 1, 2019." American Life League, 1 Mar. 2019, all.org/pro-life-this-week-03-01-2019/.

"Rape." *FBI*, FBI, 8 Oct. 2014, ucr.fbi.gov/crime-in-the-u.s/2013/crime-in-t he-u.s.-2013/violent-crime/rape.

"Reconquest of Spain." *History.com*, A&E Television Networks, 9 Feb. 2010, www.history.com/this-day-in-history/reconq uest-of-spain.

Stone, Brad. "Amazon's Escape From New York." *Bloomberg.com*, Bloomberg, 15 Feb. 2019, www.bloomberg.com/news/articles/2019-02 -14/how-amazon-lost-new-york.

Sommers, Christina Hoff. "The Gender Wage Gap Myth and 5 Other Feminist Fantasies." *Time*, Time, 2 Sept. 2014, time.com/3222543/wage-pay-gap-myth-fem inism/.

"The Equal Pay Act of 1963." *The Equal Pay Act of 1963 (EPA)*, U.S. Equal Employment Opportunity Commission, www.eeoc.gov/laws/statutes/epa.cfm.

Warning Signs of Mental Illness, www.psychiatry.org/patients-families/gender -dysphoria/what-is-gender-dysphoria.

Books

Academic American Encyclopedia. 1980.

Friedan, Betty. *The Feminine Mystique.* New York London, W. W . Norton & Company, 2013.

Hull, N. E., and Peter C. Hoffer. *Roe v. Wade The Abortion Rights Controversy in American History.* University Press of Kansas, 2001.

Documents

Haas, Ann P, et al. "Suicide Attempts among Transgender and Gender Non-Conforming Adults Findings of the National Transgender Discrimination Survey." The Williams Institute, Jan. 2014.

Ocasio-Cortez, Alexandria. "H. Res. 109 'Green New Deal.'" GPO, 7 Feb. 2019, https://www.congress.gov/116/bills/hres109/ BILLS-116hres109ih.pdf

www.ingramcontent.com/pod-product-compliance
Lightning Source LLC
Chambersburg PA
CBHW061501250726

48657CB00005B/1692